THE LITTLE BOOK OF
FREEMASONRY

© 2004 by The Book Laboratory® Inc.

This 2004 edition published by Fall River Press,
by arrangement with The Book Laboratory® Inc.

Book design by Kristen Garneau

Fall River Press
122 Fifth Avenue
New York, NY 10011

ISBN: 978-0-7607-5449-8

Printed and bound in Singapore

3   5   7   9   10   8   6   4   2

THE LITTLE BOOK OF
FREEMASONRY

SANGEET DUCHANE

FALL RIVER PRESS

Table of Contents

Introduction

Freemasonry is a fraternity that has existed since the seventeenth century. Though there have been related social organizations for women, Freemasonry has remained a fraternity, an organization of brethren. The Freemason Lodge was created to act as a kind of mystery school, where the brothers could come together and assist each other in their spiritual development and pass on ancient wisdom. Its members call Freemasonry the Craft.

Freemasonry emerged as a form of deism, which in this case means a belief in a Creator God, called The Great Architect of the Universe or T.G.A.O.U. Freemasonry does not concern itself with the details of how different groups see that Creator in Judaism, Christianity, Islam, Hinduism, or any other religion. Jehovah, God the Father, Allah, and Brahma are equally acceptable as perceptions of T.G.A.O.U.

Freemasonry emerged at a time of great religious discord, when the most common belief shared by rival religious groups was that anyone who disagreed with them should be killed in the most painful and grotesque way possible. Seeing the enormous loss of life and waste of resources in this conflict, Freemasons vowed to ban discussions of religious differences and to focus on using the resources of all the Wisdom traditions for their own personal development.

Origins of Freemasonry

One of the most common questions asked about Freemasonry is where it come from? What are its origins? This is a question hotly debated within Freemasonry itself. There are two traditional theories, and those theories are not really inconsistent with each other. The first is that the Freemasons are a secret continuation of the Knights Templar from the fourteenth century, and the second is that Freemasons are a continuation of the trade guilds of medieval builders. A more recent theory is that Freemasonry arises out of a combination of various strains of metaphysical or occult thought that came together in seventeenth-century Europe. The correct answer to the question of where Freemasonry came from is most probably, all of the above. It is likely that all of these influences—the Knights Templar, the mason guilds, and metaphysical thought—had an influence on the development of Freemasonry.

Knights Templar

The Order of the Poor Knights of Christ and the Temple of Solomon was founded in Jerusalem by Hugues de Payen sometime between 1115 and 1118. The Templars were housed in a portion of the royal palace that was built on the site of Solomon's original Temple. They were also given access to the caves under the old Temple, purportedly to stable their horses, but many believe they excavated there. If so, they may have unearthed treasure and texts. The Copper Scroll, a text actually engraved on thin sheets of copper and part of the texts found in the Dead Sea area, says that the Jews buried several caches of treasure. This information gives credence to the legend that the Templars found treasure and/or documents buried under the Temple site.

The Templars explored many avenues of knowledge in the Middle East, opening diplomatic relations with the Saracens and translating various Arabic

manuscripts. They had many preceptories or monasteries around Europe and the Middle East, and the carvings in those buildings show that the Templars knew about astrology, alchemy, sacred geometry, numerology, and astronomy. These were questionable areas of knowledge for Christians of that time, and the legendary Templar rules of secrecy may have been created to guard the order against charges of heresy.

People in recent times have found, and continue to find, early Christian documents like the Gnostic Gospels and alternative Jewish documents like the Dead Sea Scrolls. It is very likely that the Templars also found documents that did not match the Bible and the official teachings of the Church. We know that there were many more gospels and early Christian writings than actually made it into the New Testament. Many of the recently discovered texts have confused and sometimes shocked modern scholars. We can only imagine what effect similar texts might have had on people in the more literal age of the Templars. At a time when the Church was claiming the right to be the ruler of the world, based on a literal interpretation of the Bible, alternative texts would have been very dangerous to its claims.

The Templars, like all the Christians in the Holy Land at that time, also enthusiastically sought holy relics, from artifacts like the dishes of the Last Supper, a piece of the cross, or fragments of clothing, to human relics from

various saints. Some believe the Templars had custody of the Shroud of Turin for some time.

The Order of the Knights Templar captured the romantic imagination of the time, and men from many noble houses joined, donating their property. Others donated additional property, until the Templars were one of the richest bodies in Europe, financing whole kingdoms. These financial dealings would eventually lead them into trouble.

The Christian kingdom in Jerusalem was lost in 1137, partly due to poor decisions by the Templar Grand Master of that time, and the Christians were slowly pushed out of the Middle East. By that time other military religious orders such as the Teutonic Knights and the Hospitallers had been formed and had established themselves somewhere in Europe. When the Templars lost their holdings in the Middle East, they were without a real base. They had a lot of land and many preceptories throughout Europe, but did not control any territory.

The Templars became medieval diplomats, international advisors, bankers, and counselors. By the early fourteenth century, many countries owed them a great deal of money, including the French government of Philippe IV of France. Philippe had a creative alternative to paying his debts. He managed, probably by murdering an earlier pope, to get his puppet

Clement V in control of the Church, and all the Templars then in France were arrested in 1307 as heretics.

The arrests were followed by an inquisition into the orthodoxy of the order, and the order was disbanded in 1312. There was interesting testimony from some Templars, but the credibility of the testimony is undermined by the fact that it was all obtained under torture or the threat of torture. The Templars were accused of spitting on the cross and worshipping a head called Baphomet, among other heresies.

The Templars in France who were captured were tried and many were imprisoned or burned alive. In 1314 the last Grand Master of the Templars and the preceptor of Normandy were roasted to death over a slow fire. Legend says that the Master, Jacques de Molay, called on Clement and Phillipe to meet him before the throne of God within a year to account for their actions. Clement was dead within a month and Phillipe within a year. These deaths may have been helped along by Templars or their supporters, but they greatly increased the fame of the Templars and the belief in their magical powers.

Not all the Templars in France were captured. They seem to have had prior warning, and a group escaped from the Paris preceptory with the main library and treasury of the order. This group appears to have gone to the northern French coast and to have escaped on the Templar fleet, which was never

found. Templars in other countries were not treated as badly as those in France, and many survived. Portugal acquitted the Templars and gave refuge to those escaping from other areas. In Britain the king was so slow to arrest the Templars that all those who wanted to escaped and only the old and infirm were tried. Most of those were sentenced to retirement in a monastery.

There was one country that did not arrest the Templars at all: Scotland. Robert Bruce, the king of Scotland, had been excommunicated for killing an opponent in a church and had neither the inclination nor the time to be bothered with fighting the enemies of the Church.

Bruce took power by winning a major battle against the English at Bannockburn in 1314, seven years after the escape of many Templars from France and other countries. Some claim that Bruce's army was strengthened by the fighting skills and weaponry of the Templars, and it is entirely possible that the Templar fleet could have sailed to Ireland and then on to Scotland.

There is no doubt that many Templars survived the dissolution of the order and that they settled in various parts of Europe. Did they set up a secret organization to pass their teachings on?

Templars and Freemasons

An excavation of the Templar castle of Athlit in the Holy Land has showed that the Templars had their own masons, and in at least one case they carved a mason's square and a plumb stone on the tombstone of a Templar mason. Another tombstone had an anchor, indicating the captain of a ship. Most Templar tombstones had a sword, with no name, since the knight resigned his identity when he joined the order. Tombstones have been found in Scotland that have a sword and no name, and stones that have a sword and masonic symbols. Some believe that these stones indicate not only that the Templars were in Scotland but that they had a strong connection with the masons there.

The Scottish family of Sinclair (formerly Saint-Clair and related to the French family of that name) was close to the kings of Scotland, including

Robert Bruce. If the Templars did join Bruce's army, they probably would have known William Sinclair as well as the king himself. In 1441, the Scottish king James II appointed a later Sinclair, Sir William, the Patron and Protector of Scottish masons. This was a position that the family came to think of as hereditary, and the family was involved with building and with masons for many generations.

In 1446 Sir William began construction of Rosslyn Chapel. He had intended it to be a collegiate church, but after 40 years of construction on the Chapel, his son did not continue the project, and only the chapel was ever built. Rosslyn Chapel, though superficially Christian, is full of pagan symbolism, showing that Sir William had an interest in matters unusual for the time and unusual for a Christian. Legend says that Sir William imported masons from the Continent and the town of Roslin was built to accommodate them. Legends about the construction of Rosslyn later became part of Freemasonry. If masons did come from the Continent, they may have brought with them the legends and building lore they had inherited from the Roman traditions and those may have combined with the Templar's own masonic lore.

When Freemasonry became a speculative organization instead of a trade guild in the seventeenth century, the Sinclair family was involved and has

continued to be involved in Scottish Freemasonry. There was a continuity of the Sinclair family from the time that the Templars would have arrived, to the time of the masons trade guilds, to the time of speculative Freemasonry. This has contributed to belief that the Templars were the precursors of Freemasonry and to the belief that the Templar library and treasury are or were buried at Rosslyn Chapel.

There are also some similarities between what is known of the Templars and the practices of Freemasons. One point is that the only decoration that was allowed on the clothing of Templars was sheepskin, and Templars were required to wear a girdle of white sheepskin at all times as a symbol of chastity. Freemasons wear an apron of white sheepskin as a symbol of a pure life. Templar chaplains wore gloves at all times outside of Mass, to keep their hands clean for touching the Sacrament. Freemasons wear gloves as part of their rituals, and this practice began at a time in history when glove wearing was not so common as it later became. Templar proceedings were entirely secret, and it said that severe punishments were inflicted on those who violated that secrecy. Freemason rites are also secret, and Masons take oaths of secrecy that include descriptions of horrible punishments for violation of the oaths.

One objection to the theory that the Templars are the source of Freemasonry is that stories about the Templars often fail to take into account that all members of the order were not the same. There were actually three divisions in the order. The Knights came from the nobility, and like most members of the European nobility of the period, were usually illiterate. The Knights wore white mantles with a red cross, short hair, and long beards. The Knights formed the order's fighting force.

The second group of Templars was made up of the sergeants. These men were drawn from the free middle class of relatively wealthy merchants or artisans. Sergeants wore black or dark brown mantles with a red cross. They served as the men-at-arms, sentries, grooms, stewards, and other related roles.

The last group consisted of the clerics, priests, and chaplains, and these were often the only members of the order who were literate. They wore green mantles with a red cross. They were the scribes, record keepers, and librarians. They would have been the keepers of the Templar knowledge.

Given these divisions in the Templar order, the presence of Templar Knights in an area after the dissolution of the order would not guarantee the presence of any sophisticated Templar knowledge. In order to transmit Templar knowledge, the Knights would have to bring the order's documents or be accompanied by clerics. Either or both may have happened in Scotland, since the Templar library disappeared from the Paris preceptory and was

taken somewhere. The presence of some Templars in Scotland is virtually certain. The presence of particular Templar knowledge is much more difficult to demonstrate.

Operative Masonry

Stonemasons involved in the building trade are called operative masons, while Freemasons are called speculative Masons. Operative masonry was not a simple trade, but was developed into a fine art in the Greek and Roman cultures. Vitruvius, a Roman architect and thinker of the first century B.C.E., created what he called the orders of architecture, and his work and writings on architecture were influenced by the Dionysian mystery tradition. Vitruvius believed that in addition to possessing technical skills, architects should be students of philosophy, music, astrology, and similar subjects. The ideas of Vitruvius and his successors were transmitted into Europe when the Roman Empire was extended there.

When the Romans left Britain in the fourth century, the Anglo-Saxon invasion destroyed most of the stone buildings from the Roman era and building was done in wood and thatch for the next three centuries. Major building projects in stone began again around 1000, but it is unlikely that the Roman expertise could have survived in Britain during that time. It most likely did survive on the Continent, though, and there was some exchange of ideas between masons on the Continent and in Norman Britain. We can assume that at least part of the Roman building tradition made its way back into Britain when stonemasonry returned.

By the thirteenth century there were still few stone buildings being built in England. Only cathedrals, churches, and castles built by the king or by those nobles who had the king's permission to "castellate," were built of stone. Stonemasons, therefore, were employed only by the Church or the nobility, and there was a long-term connection between these groups that would surface again in the formation of Freemasonry. Masons were sometimes drafted by the king and nobles to build castles and fortifications for war, so very few masons were able to focus solely on the more artistic work of the Church. Part of what we know about the lifestyle of stonemasons is from the sculptures they made of themselves and left on buildings.

Stonemasons had different levels of expertise. They varied from the rough masons who laid ordinary hard stone, to highly skilled artisans who worked softer chalky stone, called freestone. These skilled workers were called free-stone masons, and eventually freemasons. As the stone buildings of the past

demonstrate, European stonemasons were not mere bricklayers. Some were also involved in architecture and were knowledgeable in the geometry needed to design and build intricate structures, including fantastic cathedrals. One of the mason's most valuable secrets was the secret of the keystone, the stone that made massive and intricate arches stand.

In the fourteenth and perhaps as early as the thirteenth century various trade unions were formed in England, as well as several other countries in Europe. These trade guilds were run by organizations with a charter from the king. The guilds regulated all aspects of life. The mason's guild required the members to believe in doctrines of the Catholic Church and to reject all heresies, to fulfill all duty to the king and to other superiors, and to live a moral life. Adultery, fornication, staying out after eight at night, and frequenting inns and brothels were all forbidden. Cards could only be played during the 12 days of Christmas.

After the plague or Black Death decimated Europe in the fourteenth and fifteenth centuries there was a shortage of labor. Laborers in England naturally used the shortage to their advantage and sought higher wages. In response, laws were passed limiting wages for various types of work. Many masons refused to follow these regulations and joined illegal trade unions where they agreed not to work at rates below those set by the union. Secrecy

was essential for these groups, since both the masons and their employers would be liable for high fines if they were caught. This may have been one source of the secrecy rules that later became such an important part of Freemasonry.

By the next century the operative masons had a well-developed collection of legends relating to the trade, including legends about Solomon's Temple, God as the architect of the universe, and various hermetic and Neoplatonic ideas that were not common in Europe until the Renaissance. How these ideas got into the building guilds is impossible to determine from the information we have. A popular theory is that they came from Templar influence. Like other craft guilds, the masons also participated in acting out mystery plays for the community on feast days, probably including plays that related to the building of the original Temple in Jerusalem, a practice that may have carried over into the rituals of Freemasonry.

In Scotland the operative masons were still active in guilds at the time that they began to invite speculative Masons from the upper classes to join them. In England the operative guilds were less active, and it is unclear whether there was a direct transition from operative to speculative Masonry. It is clear that the speculative Masons who began to meet in groups called Lodges in the seventeenth century took their name and their group regulations or constitutions from the earlier operative masons.

Freemasonry as a whole clearly took on many of the legends of the operative masons and used operative masonry as the basis for the symbolism and allegory it uses to teach the principals of Freemason thought.

Metaphysical Thought

Most metaphysical or esoteric thought came into Western Europe from the East. The ironic thing about its spread in Europe is that this thought, which formed a basis for religious tolerance, was spread through religious intolerance and persecution.

One of the earliest incursions of that thought into Europe began in the seventh and eighth centuries, when Islamic invaders occupied the Iberian

Peninsula and part of France. From 732 to 1492 Spain was the repository of esoteric knowledge from Islam, Judaism, classical Greek philosophy, and the whole history of the Eastern Wisdom tradition.

There was travel between Spain and other parts of Europe, and this information spread. The Bavarian knight Wolfram von Eschenbach wrote his Grail story *Parzival*—that later formed the basis of Wagner's Opera *Parsifal*—based on a story he says he found in Spain. Nicolas Flamel, the most famous Western alchemist, was said to have learned his secrets from a book he got in Spain. In 1492 when Catholic monarchs took power, banished the Jews, and began the Spanish Inquisition, many refugees fled into the rest of Western Europe, taking their information with them.

In 1493 Constantinople and the last surviving remnants of the old Byzantine Empire fell to Turkish invaders, and refugees fled to Western Europe with their libraries and texts on hermeticism, Neoplatonism, gnosticism, kabbalah, astrology, alchemy, and sacred geometry.

In Western Europe the Renaissance was beginning. Academies were set up in Italy for Byzantine studies. Sacred geometry was no longer just for architecture, but artists like Leonardo and Botticelli applied it to painting and sculpture, while others applied it to poetry, music, and theater. Platonic and

Neoplatonic teachings spread throughout Europe, including Plato's *Timaeus,* which speaks of the Creator who is the architect of the universe.

In England esoteric thought was also popular with notables such as Sidney, Spenser, Marlowe, and Francis Bacon. "Secret societies" began to form. At about the same time the Rosicrucians, a group of diests who advocated religious tolerance, formed in Germany. In 1617 the 30 Years War between Catholics and Protestants broke out, and many Rosicrucians fled to other parts of Europe.

By the seventeenth century, when Protestantism had spread and many people began to read the Bible, there was a great interest in esoteric aspects of Bible stories, such as the story of building Solomon's Temple. Theologians, philosophers, and even mathematicians wrote lengthy and scholarly texts. Isaac Newton wrote several books about Solomon's Temple. He thought Solomon was the greatest philosopher of all time and said that the Newtonian laws of gravity had been based in part on the measurements of Solomon's Temple. Newton also thought that the measurements of the Temple foresaw the second coming of Christ in 1948.

A look at Freemasonry and its symbolism shows that it borrowed quite a lot from these various traditions. Scottish masons and aristocracy may well have preserved Templar lore, and Freemasonry was clearly set up according

to the structure of operative masonry, but it is equally true that the intellectuals who became involved in speculative Freemasonry in the seventeenth and eighteenth centuries had been exposed to centuries of Eastern thought that probably resembled much of what the Templars gathered in the East. It would be impossible to single out any one source as the originator of Freemasonry.

History of European Freemasonry

The Old Charges or organizational rules from operative masonry date back to the thirteenth or fourteenth centuries, but the first records of a speculative organization did not appear until the sixteenth. The first written record of an initiation into Freemasonry was the initiation of Elias Asmole (also spelled Ashmole) in 1646. Since he was initiated into an existing Lodge, other initiations must have happened before that.

Asmole was an alchemist, astrologer, and Rosicrucian, as well as a Freemason, and is known for the Asmolean Museum at Oxford that was named for the collection Asmole left to the university. Asmole was one of the early members of the Royal Society. His fellow Royal Society member Sir Robert Moray was also a Freemason, and Christopher Wren was initiated, though he does not appear to have participated. Isaac Newton had similar interests, but was not a Freemason.

The first Grand Lodge of Freemasonry was established in London on June 24, 1717. From an early date Freemasonry in England was tied to royalty and the aristocracy. In 1787 His Royal Highness George, Prince of Wales, was initiated; he became Grand Master in 1791. He resigned the position when he became king, but others from the aristocracy followed in his footsteps. The Duke of Sussex was a Grand Master in 1814. Kings Edward VII and George VI were both Freemasons, and George VI was made a past Grand Master in 1937. In the 1960s and 1970s, several dukes were initiated, and the Duke of Kent became Grand Master in 1967.

The policy of English Freemasonry was that religious and political arguments were banned from the Lodge. It was a place of brotherhood and tolerance of varying points of view. Nonetheless, the English Grand Lodge was vocal in its support of England's war against France and general issues of loyalty to England.

Freemasonry spread throughout Europe and the rest of the world, but the eighteenth century was a difficult time for Freemasonry in much of Europe. In 1738 Pope Clement XII issued a Bull against Freemasonry. Why, he asked, would there be secrecy if they were not doing something wrong? He condemned and excommunicated all Freemasons and declared them the "enemies of the Roman Church." Popes through Leo XIII at the end of the

nineteenth century continued to issue denunciations of Freemasonry, and in 1917 Canon Law decreed excommunication for Masonic membership. There was a brief move toward tolerance after Vatican II, but Pope John Paul II has backtracked. Membership in Freemasonry is no longer considered a basis for excommunication, but it is still sinful for Catholics and can result in religious penalties.

This attitude by the Church has had a negative effect on Freemasonry in Catholic countries such as Spain, Portugal, and Latin America. The Spanish dictator Franco banned Freemasonry in 1936, and in 1940 it became illegal in Spain even to have a relative who was a Mason. Anyone related to a Mason was presumed to have "allowed" them to join, and several relatives were sentenced to long prison terms.

Also, in the eighteenth century a Bavarian secret society called the Illuminati was exposed. Confiscated writings showed a plot to foment revolution and take over Europe, if not the world. Freemasons were confused with Illuminati and a certain amount of hysterical opposition to both resulted. Accusations that the Freemasons want to take over the world are still spread across the Internet.

A very real fear arose among European monarchs when the French people revolted in 1789 and eventually executed the king and queen and much of the

French aristocracy. Freemasonry was blamed for the revolution, even though the rebels themselves had denounced Freemasonry because it was hierarchal and all members were not equal. No doubt some Freemasons supported the revolutionary cause, but like all other major conflicts of the times, there were Freemasons on both sides.

Napoleon revived Freemasonry after he took control of France. When he came to the battle of his downfall at Waterloo, most of the commanders on both sides of the battle were Freemasons.

In twentieth-century anti-Semitism Freemasons were accused of being Jewish accomplices. Freemasonry had always been open to Judaism, as well as Christianity, and used many symbols and legends from Jewish history. Freemasonry became illegal in Nazi Germany. In Botha's apartheid government in South Africa, Freemasonry was accused of aiming to establish a world government and world religion. In the 1990s some Croatians blamed Freemasons for delays in peacekeeping actions by various governments.

Though Freemasonry on the Continent has had a rocky history, it continues to thrive. Freemasonry in Britain has never had such a difficult time and continues to be connected to the royalty, aristocracy, and establishment.

GIFT RECEIPT

Barnes & Noble Booksellers #2715
731 N San Fernando Blvd.
Burbank, CA 91502
818-558-1383

STR:2715 REG:008 TRN:9261 CSHR:Edward O

Rule by Secrecy: Hidden
  9780060931841
  (1 @ RT.HH)   RT.HH G
Skeptic's Guide to Consp
  9781605501130
  (1 @ RW.HT)   RW.HT G
Little Book of Freemason
  9780760754498
  (1 @ Z.HL)   Z.HL G
Freemasonry: Its History
  9781435108226
  (1 @ RP.HL)   RP.HL G
Alchemy & Mysticism
  9783836517690
  (1 @ B.HL)   B.HL G

Thanks for shopping at
Barnes & Noble

V101.19   12/11/2009 01:32PM

CUSTOMER COPY

Return Policy

With a sales receipt, a full refund in the original form of payment will be issued from any Barnes & Noble store for returns of new and unread books (except textbooks) and unopened music/DVDs/audio made within (i) 14 days of purchase from a Barnes & Noble retail store (except for purchases made by check less than 7 days prior to the date of return) or (ii) 14 days of delivery date for Barnes & Noble.com purchases (except for purchases made via PayPal). A store credit for the purchase price will be issued for (i) purchases made by check less than 7 days prior to the date of return, (ii) when a gift receipt is presented within 60 days of purchase, (iii) textbooks returned with a receipt within 14 days of purchase, or (iv) original purchase was made through Barnes & Noble.com via PayPal. Opened music/DVDs/audio may not be returned, but can be exchanged only for the same title if defective.

After 14 days or without a sales receipt, returns or exchanges will not be permitted.

Magazines, newspapers, and used books are not returnable. *Product not carried by Barnes & Noble or Barnes & Noble.com will not be accepted for return.*

Policy on receipt may appear in two sections.

Return Policy

With a sales receipt, a full refund in the original form of payment will be issued from any Barnes & Noble store for returns of new and unread books (except textbooks) and unopened music/DVDs/audio made within (i) 14 days of purchase from a Barnes & Noble retail store (except for purchases made by check less than 7 days prior to the date of return) or (ii) 14 days of delivery date for Barnes & Noble.com purchases (except for purchases made via PayPal). A store credit for the purchase price will be issued for (i) purchases made by check less than 7 days prior to the date of return, (ii) when a gift receipt is presented within 60 days of purchase, (iii) textbooks returned with a receipt within 14 days of purchase, or (iv) original purchase was made through Barnes & Noble.com via PayPal. Opened music/DVDs/

Famous British Freemasons

Britain has had many famous Masons. Sir Winston Churchill joined the Freemasons in 1901 at the age of 26. Cecil Rhodes was also a member. In the entertainment industry, both W.S. Gilbert and Sir Arthur Sullivan of Gilbert and Sullivan fame were Freemasons, as were actors David Garrick and Peter Sellers. Many of the best known and best loved British writers were also Freemasons: Alexander Pope, Jonathan Swift, Robert Burns, Sir Walter Scott, Anthony Trollope, Oscar Wilde, Sir Arthur Conan Doyle, and Rudyard Kipling.

History of American Freemasonry

Freemasonry came to America with the British settlers, and many of the first Lodges were military Lodges in the British army. The regalia and equipment of each Lodge was portable and would travel with the company that made up the Lodge. These Lodges were under the jurisdiction of the English Grand Lodge, with some higher degrees under the warranty of the Irish Grand Lodge.

Lodges were also set up in the colonial cities like Boston and Philadelphia. Benjamin Franklin, for example, joined the Lodge in Philadelphia in 1731. At first these Lodges met in public buildings, such as the upstairs room in local inns. Because the proceedings were secret, many others tried to eavesdrop, and it was sometimes difficult to keep the curious out. Lodge buildings were later erected, but they were much simpler than the elaborate European Lodges of the time. Because Freemasonry was a moral organization and members were screened for their character, business owners sometimes used Masonic symbols in advertising to assure the public of their reliability.

Revolutionary War

When the Revolutionary War began, Freemasonry did not play a role, since there were Freemasons on both sides of the battle. George Washington, the Revolutionary Commander in Chief was a Freemason, as were most of the British commanders and many of the officers in both armies. In fact, at least one historian claims that the British did not fight as effectively as they were capable of fighting, because of the feelings of fellowship with the colonial settlers. This would have included joint membership in Freemason Lodges under the English Grand Lodge. On the other hand, no one claims that the Revolutionary forces held back for that reason.

Freemasons claimed credit for the Boston Tea Party, in which tea was taken from a ship and thrown into Boston harbor in protest of a British tax on tea. The Freemasons, however, were not the only group to claim credit for the Boston Tea Party. The Sons of Liberty also claimed credit, and many historians think they have the better claim. The colonials were opposed to taxation without representation, and their position was consistent with England's ideas of a constitutional monarchy. England insisted on imposing taxes and other restrictions without representation, and war eventually broke out.

Freemasons did play a number of important roles in the revolutionary drama. Paul Revere, the silversmith who made the fateful ride to warn the countryside of the British attack, was a Freemason. John Paul Jones, the revolutionary commander of a U.S. warship was another. He is famous for the sea battle in 1779 off New England, where he and his crew continued to fight even though their ship was sinking beneath them. When the British commander yelled across and asked Jones if he was ready to surrender, he replied, "I have not yet begun to fight." The British ship eventually surrendered and Jones won the battle.

On the other hand, Benedict Arnold, the most famous traitor of the Revolutionary War was also a Freemason. Arnold agreed to give his command, West Point, to the British forces in exchange for 10,000 pounds and a British military commission. A courier was captured with damaging documents before this could happen, and Arnold was able to escape. He was

rewarded by the British, but never trusted. His Freemason Lodge in Connecticut expelled him.

Although Thomas Paine, the freethinker whose pamphlet *Common Sense* helped to instigate the signing of the Declaration of Independence was not a Freemason, he was very interested in Freemasonry and wrote a book about it. Paine argued that parliamentary representation on issues such as taxation would not be enough to resolve difficulties between the Crown and the colonies, since America and England had drifted too far apart. America needed to declare its independence; this was simply common sense. He would later become an advocate for the French Revolution as well.

John Hancock, who signed the Declaration of Independence in very large letters, was a Freemason. Hancock had been told that the British had offered a reward for revolutionaries, so he signed in a large flamboyant script, and said that since the British commission would be able to read his signature without spectacles, they could double the reward.

A New Government

The claim is often made that Freemasonry influenced the formation of the new Union, and that is true. Though it probably had little influence on the war itself, Freemasonry had a major influence on the people who wrote the Constitution and set up the new government. By the time that the Revolutionary War was finished, organizations like the Sons of Liberty had faded, and Freemasonry had become the leading fraternal organization.

The new Constitution was written by Thomas Jefferson, but the contents were determined by the Constitutional Convention of 1787. The delegates were Jefferson, Washington, Franklin, John Adams, and Edmund Randolf. Jefferson was not a Freemason, but the majority, Washington, Franklin, and Randolf, were Freemasons. Adams was not a Freemason, but tended to side with them against Jefferson. There is no doubt that the U.S. Constitution, the document that has so much influence on American life, was heavily influenced by the principles of Freemasonry that those men took so seriously.

The story of the dedication of the Capitol building in Washington, D.C. illustrates the role that Freemasonry played at that time. The ritual was conducted by the Grand Lodge of Maryland, and George Washington was asked to serve as Master for the event.

The Lodge members, including Washington, came in full Freemason regalia, and Washington was given a silver plate inscribed with the names of all the Freemason Lodges in attendance. He placed that plate and another plate with Masonic symbols and containers of corn, wine, and oil under the cornerstone. A Freemason ceremony followed, complete with Masonic chanting.

The gavel, silver trowel, square, and level used in the ceremony are still at the Potomac Lodge No. 5 in the District of Columbia.

The Great Seal

A question often raised is whether the Seal of the United States that appears on the back of the one-dollar bill is a Freemason design. A few hours after the Declaration of Independence was signed on July 4, 1772, a committee to design a national seal was appointed. The committee consisted of Benjamin Franklin, a Freemason, and John Adams and Thomas Jefferson, who were not Freemasons. Their relationship to Freemasonry is irrelevant, however, because they failed to produce an acceptable design. After a few more committees and many changes, a design was finally accepted by Charles Thomson, Secretary of the Continental Congress, who was not a Freemason.

The half of the Seal on the left side of the bill has a pyramid with a blazing Eye of Providence in the triangle at the top of the pyramid. The year the Declaration of Independence was signed is shown in Roman numerals at the base of the pyramid. Above the design it says, "Annuit Cœptis," translated as, "It [the Eye of Providence] has favored our undertaking." On a banner underneath are the words, "Novus Ordo Seclorum," translated as "A New Order of the Ages." This probably refers to a line of Virgil that has been translated to something like, "A mighty order of the ages begins anew."

Freemasons vehemently deny that this side of the Great Seal is a Freemason design. They are concerned because this design as been used to "prove" that Freemasons control the U.S. government and the banner text has been translated as "A New World Order," with sinister implications. The truth is that there is no evidence the people actually involved in designing and selecting the seal were Freemasons or connected with Freemasonry in any way.

Though several Freemason legends refer to Egypt and Egyptian knowledge, the pyramid has never been a Freemason symbol. Freemasonry uses a triangle, containing some reference to the Deity as a symbol of God, but they borrowed that symbolism from other traditions. The same is true of the Heavenly Eye, which Freemasons call the All-Seeing Eye and the Seal designers called the Eye of Providence. This was a very common hermetic symbol and was in widespread use in the eighteenth century. One of the most famous uses of the symbol of the single eye was the Egyptian Eye of Horus.

There is no evidence that the Seal contains actual Freemason symbols, but it clearly contains symbols that Freemasons shared with others in that time. It is fair to say that the designers of the national seal shared some of the ideas of Freemasonry, which resulted in some similarities of symbolism.

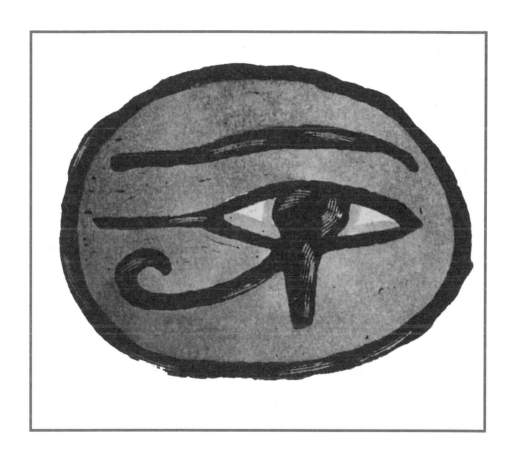

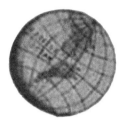

From Independence to Scandal

Many Freemasons seemed more concerned about declaring independence from the Grand Lodge of England than from the King and Parliament. Eventually, however, independence was declared, and each state, like each European nation, established its own Grand Lodge. Different rites were developed from those used in Europe, and American Freemasonry began to take on a form of its own.

In the early days of the Republic Freemasonry was highly thought of and grew quickly. In America Freemasonry became more Christian than it had been in Europe, and, despite the liberality of early Freemason teachings, was racially segregated. An African American, Prince Hall, established black Freemasonry in the United States. Freemasonry is no longer completely segregated, but there are still Lodges that do not recognize Prince Hall Masonry.

The reputation of Freemasonry was seriously damaged by a scandal in 1826. William Morgan, a resident of upstate New York, joined the Freemasons and either became disgruntled or intended to spy from the very beginning. He left the Lodge and announced that he had written a book, *Illustrations of Masonry,* which he was going to have published, and that the book would reveal secret Masonic rituals.

Morgan was kidnapped by a group of Masons and was never seen again. Since there was no body, murder could not be proven and the Masons were charged with misdemeanors. There were 20 trials and three successive special prosecutors, but Freemasons were on the juries and there were only a few convictions with minor jail terms.

The kidnapping and presumed murder followed by the cover-up fueled anti-Mason sentiment. Morgan's book was a bestseller, and anti-Masonic literature flourished, some satirical and some vitriolic. Thousands left Freemasonry in disgust or protest and Freemasonry languished for many years. By 1884 Freemasonry was as popular or more popular than before, but it never quite regained the position of prominence it had in earlier days.

Famous American Freemasons

In the 108 years between 1789–1897, eight out of twenty-three presidents were Freemasons: Washington, Madison, Monroe, Andrew Jackson, Polk, Buchanan, Andrew Johnson, and Garfield. In the 56 years between 1897–1953, seven out of nine presidents were Freemasons: McKinley, Theodore Roosevelt, Taft, Harding, Hoover, F.D. Roosevelt, and Truman. Since then only Lyndon Johnson and Gerald Ford have been Freemasons. Other Freemason politicians and political leaders have crossed the political spectrum. J. Edgar Hoover, Douglas MacArthur, and Fiorello La Guardia, the former mayor of New York, were all Freemasons.

Quite a few of the nineteenth century's business giants were Freemasons: John Jacob Astor, Henry Ford, Walter Chrysler, Ransom E. Olds, King C. Gillette, Alexander Horlick (chocolate milk), James C. Penney, and David Sarnoff. The same is true of several twentieth-century aviation giants: Charles Lindburgh, John Glenn, James B. Irwin, and Leroy Gordon Cooper.

The entertainment industry has had its share of Freemasons as well: Cecil B. DeMille, Louis B. Meyer, Darryl F. Zanuck, Jack L. Warner, John Philip Sousa, Irving Berlin, Louis Armstrong, Duke Ellington, Nat King Cole, and Count Basie, to name a few.

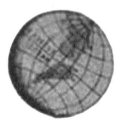

American Freemasonry Today

Freemasonry in the United States has more members and is more prosperous than in any other country. In 1998 there were more than 17,000 Lodges in the country. The majority of U.S. Lodges accept the Scottish Rite and many the York Rite. There is also a Masonic organization that is unique to the United States, founded in New York in 1870. That is The Ancient Arabic Order of Nobles of the Mystic Shrine, known more commonly as the Shriners. Only Freemasons who have reached the 32nd degree of the Scottish Rite or the Knights Templar degree in the York rite are eligible to join. The Shriners have over 500,000 members in North America (including Canada, Mexico, and Panama).

Freemasons in the United States are known for their charity work. The Shriners alone sponsor 22 hospitals that specialize in treating children under 18 free of charge for orthopedic or burn care. There are 20 hospitals in the United States and one each in Canada and Mexico.

Legends and Symbols

Freemasons' Genesis

Freemason legends reconfigured history from a Freemason point of view. According to those legends, Masonry dates from the earliest point of human time: Creation. The God of the Old Testament was the first Mason, as he created the world in six days.

Adam was a Mason, and the Masons built the Tower of Babel, and since the people spoke in different languages, God told the Masons to communicate with each other in the form of secret signs. This is the origin of the Freemason secret handshakes and gestures. Noah was also a Mason and preserved the animal and plant life forms. The knowledge that existed before the Flood, such as geometry, music, animal husbandry, and metalworking, was placed in two columns of stone and metal, and so survived flood and fire. These columns were the two main columns of Solomon's Temple. In some legends the knowledge from before the Flood was revived by Pythagoras, who was, of course, a Mason.

Abraham was a Mason and invented geometry, which is so important to masonry. In Egypt Abraham met a Greek slave named Euclid and taught geometry to him. Euclid wrote it down, and from his writings the whole world has learned geometry.

Hiram Abiff

The legend of Hiram Abiff is the most basic legend of Freemasonry, and in comes down to the present in several versions. The legend is based on the description of the building of Solomon's Temple in 1 Kings 5–7.

The legend says that when Solomon decided to build the Temple he contacted King Hiram of Tyre for materials and skilled workmen. King Hiram provided his best Master Builder, Hiram Abiff. These three principals, Solomon, King Hiram, and Hiram Abiff were the keepers of a secret word of the Temple.

In some versions that word is the secret of the Temple, and in others it is the Master's word, the word that distinguished the Master builders from the Apprentices and Fellows. With thousands of workers on the Temple, the only way for Hiram Abiff to know what to pay each of them was for each group to

have a separate word and handshake. The Apprentice word was Boaz, the Fellow word was Jochin, and the Master word was Jehovah.

Three evil workers attacked Hiram Abiff in the Temple, trying to force him to reveal the secret word. As they stabbed him, he moved from door to door, tracing a pattern in his blood on the floor. He died without revealing the secret, and the evildoers, afraid at what they had done, took his body out and buried it on a hillside. They planted a small acacia over the body to hide the disturbed earth.

When Hiram Abiff was discovered to be missing, search parties were sent out to find the body. They were fearful that Hiram Abiff may have revealed the secret word, so Solomon and King Hiram decided that the first word spoken when the body was found would be the new Master word.

One of the searchers took hold of the acacia to steady himself on the hillside. The plant came up by the roots, and the body was found. Someone grasped Hiram's hand and the skin slipped off like a glove, and the Master who had touched the hand, exclaimed, "Macbenae!" (or one of several variations). This is loosely translated as, "the flesh falls from the bone," "the flesh is rotten," and "death of a builder."

A variant of this part of the story is that Solomon declared that the first thing the searchers saw when they discovered the body would be the secret of the Temple. When they found the body and opened the coffin, the first thing they saw was the hand of Hiram Abiff, so the handshake and other Masonic signs of recognition became the new secret of the Temple.

In yet another version, Hiram Abiff wore the watchword of the Temple on a golden triangle on his chest. When he was attacked he managed to throw the triangle into a deep shaft, where seekers after the unpronounce-able name of God must go to find it. This search became part of the ritual of the Royal Arch degree.

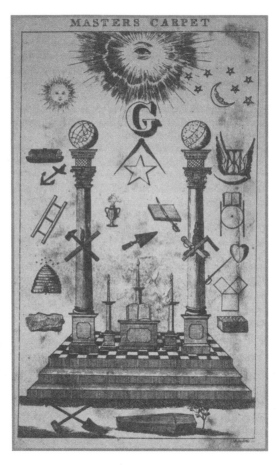

Symbols

Freemasonry has a large number of symbols. It borrowed many of them from various forms of metaphysical thought, created some, and gave new meanings to others. Many of the symbols are described to the candidates during the initiation into the three basic degrees. Though all there is to know about Freemasonry symbolism could easily fill a large volume, there are a few basic symbols that reoccur frequently and are important to the teachings of the Craft. In American Freemasonry, charts were made of all the symbols to ensure that the Lodges were using them correctly. This chart was sometimes called a Masters Carpet.

The Lodge

The Lodge itself is a symbol of the metaphysical structure of the individual and of the mystical work of Freemasonry. The physical Lodge is an assemblage of brethren and a four-sided building. The individual is an assemblage of faculties, and the square is the symbol of physical organisms. The physical world is made up of four elements, and the square is a reminder that an organism consists of all elements in balance. In almost all Western philosophical thought before the nineteenth century, both the universe and the individual human were believed to be designed according to the same four-level plan.

In the physical, as opposed to symbolic, Lodge the room where the meetings and ceremonies are held is called the Oblong Square. The Master presides from the east end. Lodges were designed symbolically, but also with an eye to secrecy. In some nineteenth-century buildings the interior chamber is surrounded by a passageway that serves as a buffer. Lodges from England to Japan reflect both the principles of Freemasonry and the cultural design of the area.

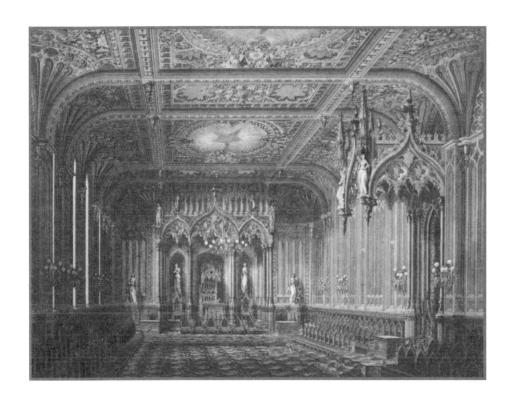

The Deity

The Creator Deity is central to Freemason thought, and some representation of the Deity appears in most Masonic charts and artwork. There are several symbols that can relate to or signify Deity, including five-pointed and eight-pointed stars, a triangle, an eye, the letter G, and the Hebrew name of God. These symbols are often associated with a glory, or aura of radiant light.

The Deity can be represented by any combination of these symbols. For example, there may be a star with a circle and triangle in the center; an eye surrounded by a glory; a triangle containing an eye surrounded by a glory; or a triangle containing the letter G or Hebrew letters for God. In Freemasonry, a five-pointed star surrounded by a glory, is often called the Glory.

Columns of the Temple

The Old Testament tells us in 1 Kings 7 that Hiram from Tyre, a skilled bronze worker, came to work on Solomon's Temple and that he cast two bronze pillars for the vestibule of the Temple. The dimensions of the pillars are different in 1 Kings 7 and II Chronicles 3. The pillar to the north was called Boaz, and the pillar to the south was called Jachin.

In Freemason legend Boaz was the father of King David and Jachin was the High Priest who helped to dedicate Solomon's Temple. Sometimes the directions of the pillars are reversed and Jachin represents the land of Israel in the north, and Boaz represents the land of Judah in the south. In another legend, these pillars contain all forms of ancient knowledge from before the Flood. They also mark off the entryway to spiritual work.

Freemasonry adds another dimension to the symbolism by adding architectural features to the columns. In Greek architecture there were three orders of architecture: Doric, Corinthian, and Ionic. Boaz and Jachin are portrayed as Doric and Corinthian columns, signifying active and passive principals, and a third Ionic column is often portrayed as well. The three columns symbolize Wisdom, Strength, and Beauty.

Skull and Crossbones

The Skull and Crossbones was a popular symbol in the seventeenth and eighteenth centuries and was not yet associated with any particular group. This frightening symbol was adopted by pirates to form the Jolly Roger flag. If the flag was black, that was dangerous, but if the flag was red, that meant the pirates would show no mercy.

Freemasons of that time also adopted the symbol, but for a very different reason. The skull and crossbones symbolized the death of the individual self or ego, the death that is required before resurrection into a higher level of being or consciousness. This symbol is also associated with physical death and appears on regalia used for funeral services. This symbol reminds us of our fragile mortality, the inevitability of death, and our ultimate accountability for our actions.

The Freemasons have several legends about the origin of the symbol. One legend says that when Hiram Abiff's body was discovered, the skull rested on crossbones. Another version attributes this symbol to a story about Robert Bruce, King of Scotland. There is also a Templar legend connected to the symbol. In that story a Templar Knight loved a woman who died. He was so possessed by his passion that he broke his vows, came to her grave, and violated the body. After he had finished a voice spoke to him from the grave, telling him to come back in nine months. When he returned and dug up the grave, he found a skull resting on the woman's thighbones. The voice told him to take the skull, and he did. The skull was magical and gave him magical advice. This story may be related to the charges that the Templars had a magical head called Baphomet that they worshiped.

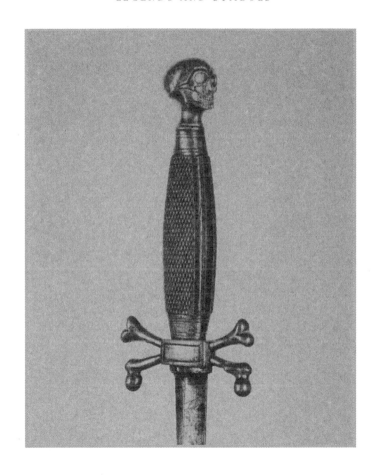

Artifacts

Floor Cloths and Tracing Boards

A chart or picture containing relevant symbols is used to initiate candidates into various degrees of Masonry. In the earliest days of Freemasonry the Tyler, a Lodge officer responsible for guarding the door, had the responsibility of drawing the necessary chart on the floor of the Lodge. Eventually the Lodge had the charts professionally painted on canvas that could be rolled up and stored when not needed for a ritual. This resulted in chipped paint after a few years, so the charts were eventually mounted on boards, sometimes hinged so that they could be stored and so that the charts would be hidden from prying eyes. The mounted charts are called tracing boards. There are different charts for the ritual for each degree.

Lodges have three items that are called the Immovable Jewels of the Lodge. Those are the rough and smooth ashlars or building stones and the tracing board. There are differences between the tracing boards that were developed in the European Freemasonry tradition and those developed in the American. American tracing boards tend to be more simple.

Regalia

The most basic piece of regalia is the Masonic apron. As we have seen, this is a white lambskin apron embroidered or painted with Masonic symbols. Many claim that the apron was worn by operative masons, but there is no evidence that operative masons used lambskin to hold their tools and materials. The use of lambskin seems to trace back to the Templar practice of wearing a white lambskin girdle.

Modern aprons are usually manufactured and indicate the Freemason's degree. Older aprons were often embroidered by the women in the Freemason families with a variety of Freemason symbols or painted by hand. Many were quite elaborate and skillfully done. Aprons are sometimes decorated in black for funeral services.

Sashes are another common item of regalia. They were traditionally used in American Freemasonry for officers of the Grand Lodge or for certain degrees in the English York Rite. All Companions of the Royal Arch Degree wear a scarlet sash with the words, "Holiness to the Lord."

White gloves were traditionally worn by all Freemasons, and are still worn by most Freemasons on some occasions. They are worn by Lodge officers at ceremonies and meetings and symbolize clean hands or a spotless, pure Masonic life.

In American Freemasonry only the Master of the Lodge wears a hat. He doffs the hat when Deity or The Great Architect of the Universe is mentioned and removes the hat while the Grand Master of the state visits the Lodge. When the superior officer leaves, the Master resumes the badge of authority.

Costumes and Uniforms

Like the ancient guilds of operative masons, Freemasons sometimes act out teaching stories comparable to the medieval mystery plays. These are metaphorical enactments for the purpose of teaching Masonic principals to degree candidates. These enactments are most common in the initiation ceremonies for the Royal Arch Degree.

In that ritual, for example, one officer of the Lodge plays the High Priest, who represents Joshua, the High Priest of the Jews. Another plays the King, representing Zerubbabel, Governor of Judah; and a third plays the Scribe, representing the prophet Haggai. In the American rite the High Priest wears a miter headdress, a sleeveless coat, and a breastplate. The King wears a crown and holds a scepter, and the Scribe wears a turban. Other minor characters in the drama wear a variety of headgear. Costuming for these rituals in past centuries was much more elaborate.

Uniforms are worn by Freemasons who join the degrees relating to military orders, such as the Knights Templar or the Red Cross Knights. The Templar uniform was originally black, but was later modified to black and white.

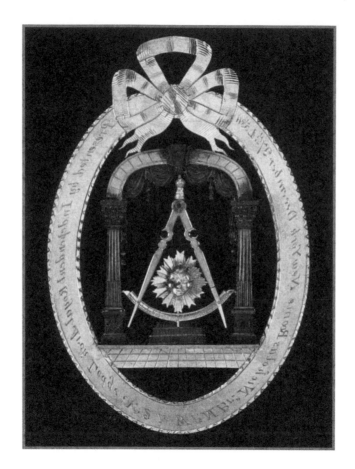

Jewels and Medals

Ceremonial medals are usually called jewels and are issued for a variety of commemorative purposes. The term "jewels" is not inappropriate in many cases, because some of the medals are remarkable examples of the jeweler's art.

Jewels are sometimes badges of office. Past Masters of a Lodge are given jewels, as are the recipients of some special degrees. Jewels were traditionally worn suspended on a silk ribbon. The ribbon sometimes came to a V on the wearer's chest, such as the ones shown in the paintings of Benjamin Franklin and George Washington, and sometimes was looped around the neck. Wearing medals and decorations on ribbons is a carryover from European tradition. Jewels were also worn on ornamental chains.

Swords

Swords are an important part of Freemason ceremonials. Swords were, of course, very important in the world of chivalry out of which Freemasonry grew. Chivalric Knights, and certainly Templar Knights, owned and were skilled in the use of swords. Swords were also used to initiate a knight. From the time of chivalry, the sword took on Christian mystic significance. The hilt formed a kind of cross, a symbolism that comes up in the Grail legends, and the bright shining blade symbolized purity of thought and deed.

In modern Freemasonry a sword is used to guard the door or portal against intruders and to preserve the confidentiality of the proceedings. Swords are also used in ritual work. For example, in one ritual the candidate feels the point of a sword against his breast, reminding him of the danger of the work he is about to undertake. The sharp point also symbolizes charity and mercy, while the double-edged blade of the sword represents the capability of Justice to cut both ways.

The military orders use swords as part of their uniforms.

Furniture

Traditionally, the "furniture" of the Lodge was the Written Word—this is usually the Holy Bible, but it could also be any other kind of scripture, such as the Torah, Qur'an, Bhagavad Gita, and so on—the Square, and the Compasses. In more recent times the primary "furniture" of the Lodge has been identified as the Mosaic Pavement, the Blazing Star, and the Indented Tarsel. The pavement is the floor of the Lodge, the star the center, and the tarsel a form of checkered border, also found around the edges of some tracing boards. The original three pieces of "furniture" are now sometimes considered secondary "furniture." The Pavement, Star, and Tarsel are also sometimes called the Ornamental.

Over the years Lodges began to accumulate furniture in the general meaning of the word, furniture for seating, writing desks, tables for refreshments, chests to store costumes, regalia, and other ritual materials, and two hollow brass pillars. These have sometimes been beautifully designed with various Freemason symbols.

Other items have also been specially designed, such as dishes for entertainment and the doorknockers necessary for those seeking entry to the Lodge.

The Entered Apprentice Degree

T his degree, which refers to the apprentice stonemason who enters the trade at the most basic level in his youth, is symbolic of the person who enters a transition from the physical life to the spiritual life. Those entering on this path are apprentices with much to learn. The candidate is symbolized by the Rough Ashlar. The ashlar is a building stone, and a rough ashlar, fresh from the quarry, is not yet ready to take its place in an edifice. It must be shaped and smoothed; its rough edges must be removed. In Freemason thought, the symbolic edifice built by polished humanity is the Temple of God. The Apprentice is entering the process to become part of the Temple of God.

This degree of Freemasonry is a preparatory degree for real entry into spiritual work. The Apprentice is expected to learn self-discipline and to symbolically purify himself for deeper work. In the ancient mystery schools an apprentice would prepare for seven years and undergo initiation for that period of time. When the physical body and emotions were no longer

disturbed, the initiate could focus on a higher level of awareness. In modern Freemasonry the candidate is only symbolically tested by assigned members of the Lodge.

The symbolism of the lessons of the Apprentice Degree is reflected in the floor cloths or tracing boards used as teaching aids for the candidates. For example, the Rough and Perfect Ashlars are often pictured in the charts for this degree.

A major feature of the First Degree board is the Checkered Pavement. The Apprentice is limited to the first floor of the Temple, and he must learn to walk on the pavement. The alternating black and white squares symbolize the world as perceived from the human perspective. The Deity perceives the Universe as part of a cohesive whole, which is symbolized by the blazing star or Glory or All Seeing Eye at the top center of the chart.

Humanity has been shattered into fragments and has lost the awareness of its true origin and nature. Humanity perceives the Universe as dualistic; parts of the Universe are at best complementary and often in opposition. The principal of duality is that whenever something is perceived as existing separate from the Divine Source, its complement also appears to provide a balance for it. When we believe these complements are in opposition to each other, we live a life of struggle and effort. The Apprentice must learn to "walk upon" opposites and find equilibrium. Though the pavement appears to be in duality, it actually fits together into one complete whole. The Apprentice learns the difference between the appearance and the reality of the ground we walk upon.

Two or three columns or pillars are also included in most tracing boards for this degree. The first two columns are Boaz and Jachin, the active and passive principals. These are sometimes balanced by a third column in the center. These pillars illustrate certain principles of geometry and symbolize the inner chamber of the Soul.

At yet another level, a more subtle form of duality is symbolized by the sun and moon, or moon and stars, that appear on either side of the Deity symbol. A ladder usually leads from the ground floor of the Temple to the heavenly realms. That ladder has three main rungs, Faith, Hope, and Charity, and these figures are often pictured sitting on the ladder. The ladder is the one Jacob sees in his vision in the Old Testament story.

At the bottom of the ladder are the Three Great Lights: the book of scripture with the Square and Compasses on top of it. The Written Word is the physical expression of the unwritten Eternal Word. The Square, in this context, symbolizes the human Soul. The Soul is created perfect, or square. The symbol for the Soul is the Water Triangle, which is a triangle with the apex pointing down. The Square is placed on the Written Word to form two sides of that triangle. The Compasses represent the animating Spirit of the Soul, or the spirit as opposed to the psyche. This aspect is represented by the Fire Triangle, which is a triangle with the apex pointing upward. The Compasses are placed on the Written Word to form two sides of that Triangle.

The point within a circle symbolizes unity and the principal of creation, while the parallel lines on either side symbolize another form of duality. In

the English Craft these represent Moses the prophet and Solomon the lawgiver. In the American system, they represent the two patron saints of Freemasonry: John the Baptist and John the Evangelist.

The tools of the First degree are the Gavel and 24-inch Gauge or Rule, and sometimes the Chisel. These may or may not be pictured with other Masonic tools in the chart. The Gavel or hammer is an active force, and the Chisel directs that force to the appropriate place. The Gauge or ruler allows one to judge. The apprentice is learning to use judgment to direct action to the purpose of transforming the rough to the smooth. The Gauge is also a measure of time and the number 24 is symbolic of a day or a complete cycle of time.

The Fellowcraft Degree

The essence of Masonic doctrine is that all men are in search of something in their own nature that they have lost. With proper instruction, patience, and industry, they can find it again. The Fellowcraft Degree is the first step in that search. While the Apprentice Degree was about initiation into the spiritual life and the work concerned with quieting the body and mind, the Fellow is now ready to look within at his own nature. This involves going up the spiral staircase to the second floor of the Temple.

The candidate for the Fellowcraft Degree is likened to a ripened Ear of Corn, which is sometimes pictured in the chart, though what is called corn is actually pictured as wheat. The candidate is ripened and ready to move to a new level. To do this the Fellow uses the winding staircase that, like the ladder in the Apprentice chart, moves in an east-west direction. This staircase of Solomon's Temple is mentioned in 1 Kings 6:8, which says: "The entrance for the middle story was on the south side of the house: one went up by winding stairs to the middle story, and from the middle story to the third."

This entrance to the second story is flanked by two columns or pillars. These are sometimes identified as the pillar of cloud and the pillar of fire. In Exodus 13:21 it says that when the Israelites escaped from Egypt and traveled in the desert, "The Lord went in front of them in a pillar of cloud by day, to lead them along the way, and in a pillar of fire by night, to give them light, so that they might travel by day and by night." The two pillars at the entrance to the second level are also identified as Wisdom and Strength. The candidate acts as the third pillar, or the pillar of Beauty or Balance.

The number of stairs in the winding stair to the second level differs in various Masonic traditions. In American Freemasonry it usually has 15 steps. The steps are divided into groups and given symbolic meanings. There are three steps in the first group, and the number three is common in the Craft. For example, there were three original Grand Masters: Solomon, King Hiram, and Hiram Abiff; there are three pillars, three Great Lights, three Immovable Jewels, and so on. The second group has five steps. Five symbolizes the pentagram, which was the symbol of Pythagoras's fraternity. The pentagram is the symbol of the human microcosm. The last group has seven steps, which symbolizes the seven Liberal Arts and Sciences at one level of understanding, and seven levels of consciousness at another.

There are some, particularly in modern Freemasonry, who interpret this second degree in a non-spiritual way, as pertaining to education. They cite the seven Liberal Arts and Sciences as evidence that this is the meaning of the degree. In ancient thought, however, the seven Liberal Arts and Sciences were an essential part of spiritual work, and education and spirituality were not separate categories as they have become in much of the modern world. The concept of seven levels of consciousness is common in mystical thought from the mysticism of Teresa of Avila to the seven chakras of Indian philosophy.

In spiritual work the ascension to the second level is a time of turning inward. The candidate enters the middle chamber of the Temple, a symbol of the Holy of Holies within each person. The tracing board or floor chart for this degree will show a symbol for Deity within the second chamber, indicating the godliness within each person. In the chamber the Fellow receives the wages of the builders of the Temple: corn, wine, and oil. The corn symbolizes nourishment and sustenance of life. At a more spiritual level it can symbolize resurrection. The wine symbolizes refreshment, health, and spiritual health. It can also symbolize mystical attainment. The oil stands for joy, gladness, and happiness. It also stands for consecration.

The tools of the second degree are the Square, the Level, and the Plumb. The Square symbolizes morality, truthfulness, and honesty. The Square makes

things straight and points the Fellow in the right direction. The Level symbolizes equality. It measures against the horizontal and stands for the quality of judgment. The Plumb symbolizes uprightness. It measures against the vertical and stands for the quality of mercy.

The tracing board or floor cloth for the Fellowcraft degree will also have a symbol representing Deity at the top, such as a triangle with a G in the middle, surrounded by a glory. G both stands for geometry and is the initial of the Deity. This symbol does not literally represent the Deity, but is a reminder that one's actions are recorded and incorporated into the fabric of existence.

Officers of the Lodge are also pictured in many boards for this degree. There are officers that correspond to each symbolic level of consciousness. The senior officers of the Lodge are considered the lights and bring wisdom to the Lodge.

This degree is also represented by the Perfect Ashlar, the building stone that has been shaped and smoothed until it is ready to take its place in an edifice. As the Fellow enters the middle chamber of the Temple, he is ready to become part of something greater than himself.

The Master Degree

The Master Degree is the real degree of a Freemason. Though higher degrees were added later, this degree was the one in which the Mason was made a full member of the Lodge, eligible to attend all its functions. No Freemason is qualified to seek higher degrees before attaining this one.

The tracing boards or floor cloths for this degree carry forward the symbolism of the earlier degrees: the checkered pavement, the two pillars in the porch of the Temple, and the winding staircase. This symbolizes that the candidate is now able to walk in the world in equilibrium and to ascend to the chamber of his inner nature. There is often a dormer window, symbolizing the light of inner knowledge to which the candidate now has access.

Tracing boards for the third degree show the outline of a coffin that contains most of the other symbols on the board. The coffin symbolizes a form of death, not physical death, but the death of the ego, the separate self that

of harmony with the plan of a greater architect. Death as initiation was a common concept in philosophy. Plutarch said, "To become initiated involves dying." In Plato's *Phaedo,* Socrates says, "The whole study of the philosopher (or wisdom seeker) is nothing else than to die and be dead."

At the Apprentice level the candidate was initiated into the physical realm. He learned how to deal with the apparent duality of physical reality and how to calm his body and mind. Now the candidate "dies to" this idea and goes beyond the world of duality into another level of functioning.

This concept is relayed to the candidate by the enactment of the death of Hiram Abiff. The death of Abiff is said to have happened when the work on the Temple was almost completed. The death of the candidate's separate self

takes place when his work on himself or his inner Temple is almost completed. The candidate is to be a Temple of God, and this can be understood on many levels.

The tools of the Master Mason are the Pencil, the Skirrett, and the Compasses. The Pencil is an action tool that symbolizes the use of creative thought. The Skirrett is a tool that constrains the pencil and can symbolize understanding, but also can mean tradition or knowledge that acts as a restraint on action. The Compasses are used to measure in all drafting and for the formation of many geometrical shapes. These tools are the tools of design and of a master architect. The role of architect is the highest role of the builder and both God and Jesus are represented using Compasses and portrayed as architects.

Having mastered all three levels of the Craft, the Master Mason can stand firmly in the physical reality of the world, look inside himself, and open himself to the Divine Will of the greatest architect.

Advanced Degrees

Degrees beyond the level of the Master Mason were developed in the eighteenth century and later, and the development of these degrees has not been consistent throughout the world. Unlike Freemasonry itself, which was to be open to anyone who believed in a deity, some of the higher degrees are only for Christians. The Knights Templar degree, for example, is a Christian degree.

The most well known higher degree is the Royal Arch degree, which was developed around 1750. Some say that it was created by the Chevalier Ramsey, an early French Freemason who insisted that Freemasonry had originated with the Knights Templar, but the Royal Arch may also have originated in Ireland. This degree takes the Master degree one step further. While the candidate for the Master degree dies to the past, the candidate for the Royal Arch degree is resurrected into the exultation of consciousness. In English Masonry many consider the Royal Arch degree as the actual completion of the Master Degree.

In the initiation ceremony for this degree, the candidate is told the name of The Great Architect of the Universe: reported to be Jabulon. According to one interpretation Jah is for Jehovah, Bul is for Baal, and On is for Osiris. In one version of the ceremony the candidate is told that this is the ineffable name of God that was revealed to Moses at the burning bush and that has laid buried under the ruins of the Temple. Initiates for the degree begin to rebuild the Temple and discover the ark of the new covenant in an underground vault where Solomon, King Hiram, and Hiram Abiff hid it when the Temple was built. The candidates open it to find a book of the law and the key to the ark symbols. There are three mysterious words, which make up the name of the deity that can only be spoken in groups of three men, forming triangles with their arms and feet. This position is referred to as the living arch, by three times three. Each participant in the arch says one syllable of the name in three languages: Jah-bul-lon; Je-ho-va; G-O-D.

The new state of one who attains this degree is symbolized by an equilateral triangle with a point in the center. The equilateral triangle symbolizes the spiritual, psychic, and physical all in balance, with the point of common life at the center. This symbol is worked in gold on the sash of Masons with this degree.

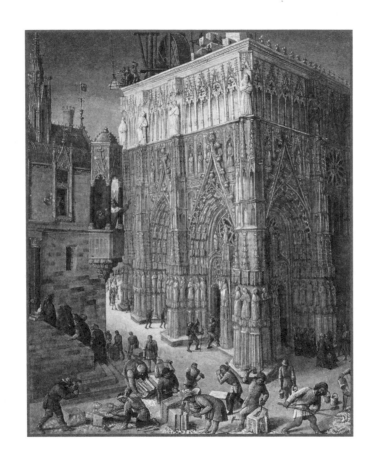

Secret Teachings

Freemasonry has often been criticized because of its secrecy, but its need for secrecy in the beginning was very real. The traditions from which Freemasonry may have arisen all had a need for secrecy. The Knights Templar needed to hide their interest in subjects the Church of their time considered heretical. The operative masons needed to hide their secret trade unions, and people interested in occult subjects had to be careful of both the Catholic and Protestant churches. Freemasonry itself insisted on religious tolerance, a position that would not have won favor with any of the warring factions. Christians and Muslims had been killing each other and the Christians had been killing Jews for centuries. By the seventeenth century Christianity had split into two warring groups, Catholics and Protestants, who were waging wars on each other all over Europe.

Freemasons also wanted to protect the secrecy of their rituals so that candidates would receive the full impact at the time of initiation. This secrecy led to a great deal of curiosity, and when meetings were held in public buildings there was a problem with eavesdroppers. One cartoon showed a chambermaid falling through a ceiling when she tried to listen in on a meeting. She ended up revealing more than the Masons did.

Secrecy was always part of Wisdom traditions. Mystery schools maintained a strict secrecy and information was revealed to initiates only when they had reached the appropriate level. This was because in authentic spiritual initiations, more than information is relayed; the initiate is given information at an energetic level. If the candidate is not properly prepared, the energetic transmission can be harmful. The secrecy, then, is to protect people from the effects of their own curiosity.

If Freemasons ever had custody of things like the Templar library, that secret is lost to Freemasons. There may be families who keep that knowledge, but it does not appear to have ever been commonly known in the Craft.

Does Freemasonry still have secret teachings? Most of the symbolism and ritual of Freemasonry has been revealed over the years, but the real secrets of Freemasonry are internal. As each candidate takes the path through his own inner being, he discovers the real secrets of Freemasonry. These are secrets that cannot be revealed; they can only be experienced.

Acknowledgments

Alexander Roob, 12, 55, 83, 122, 129, 130, 138; American Antiquarian Society, 147; Biblioteca Nationale, Florence, 133; British Library, London, 10, 14, 19, 34; British Museum, London , 9, 27, 100, 142; Charles Walker Collection, 39; Collections of the Grand Lodge of Pennsylvania, 69; Edimedia, Paris, 40; Grand Lodge Collection, 49; Grand Lodge of A.F. & A. Masons of Ireland, 77, 134; Grand Lodge of Free & Accepted Masons of Japan, 116; Historisches Museum der Tadt Wien, Vienna, 6; Hulton Picture Library, London, 66; Jerusaleum, Jewish National University Library, 43; Kilmartin Church, Argyll, 22; Museede la Ville de Paris, 52; Museum Grootoosten, The Hague, 91; Museum of Fine Arts, Boston, 61, 63; Museum of Our National Heritage, Lexington, MA, 45, 58, 74, 80, 92, 95, 97, 99, 103, 104, 107, 109, 110, 112, 115, 119, 120, 123, 124, 136, 144, 151; National Gallery of Scotland, Edinburgh, 21; Osterreichische Nationalbibliothek, Vienna, 36; Palatine Gallery, Florence, 50; Saint Catherine's Monastery, 127; St. Godehard, Hildesheim, Germany, 3; Thames and Hudson, London, 33; The Bridgeman Art Library, 148; The William Blake Trust, London, 84; Topham Picturepoint, 30; Universitatbibliothek Heidelberg, 88, 141; Yale University Art Gallery, 64.